I0791562

Check "American" and the 2020 Census

Why "American" should be the first available category for your race, creed, color and ethnicity

PETER A. THALHEIM

PAGE PUBLISHING
Conneaut Lake, PA

First Edition

PAGE PUBLISHING
Conneaut Lake, PA

First originally published by Page Publishing 2021

ISBN 978-1-6624-0912-7 (pbk)
ISBN 978-1-6624-0913-4 (digital)

Printed in the United States of America

Contents

Introduction

WHAT COLOR IS an American? There is no color, but we are a people whether we were born here or immigrated here. There is no preconceived, conventional category for any citizen. When we are asked for our race, creed, color, or ethnic background, the categories offered by the government are inherently flawed if they do not include the category of "American!" The categories offered in the 2020 census for race and ethnicity were white, black, African-American, American Indian or Alaska Native, Chinese, Filipino, Asian Indian, Vietnamese, Korean, Japanese, other Asian, Native Hawaiian, Samoan, Chamorro, other Pacific Islander, *some other race* (emphasis added), Mexican, Mexican American, Chicano, Puerto Rican, Cuban and another Hispanic, Latino or Spanish Origin. "Some other race" does not cut it for those of us who identify as American. It is long overdue that American, be inserted as the first category on any government form that asks your race, creed, color, or ethnic background.

Chapter 1

An Individual's Choice

I T IS AN individual's choice how they see themselves. If someone has immigrated to America but five years ago and feels so acclimated and attached to this great experiment in democracy, he or she should be able to mark themselves down as American. Just as the English language is the great equalizer and key to assimilation in America, the self-described label of American is a great equalizer between native born and immigrant. You can't get any higher than American.

According to the Pew Research Center, June 10, 2015, prior to 1960, the census takers would mark down the race they thought you were. Then in 1960, the citizen could choose. Starting in 2000, according to the Pew Research Center, a person could mark down more than one race. And under the guidelines of the US Census Bureau, Hispanic/Latino is not a race but is considered an ethnicity or heritage.

Chapter 2

Is America a Melting Pot or Salad Bowl?

S AN IMMIGRANT from West Germany, who had attended K-12 public schools in Connecticut and had gone to college in Vermont and law school in Cleveland, Ohio, and Durham, North Carolina, I certainly had time to acclimate from a three-year-old German immigrant to an American. So much so that after my time in the US Army Reserve, this idea of American as a unifying concept had made its mark. You may recall from your junior high school class or middle school history class that they asked whether America was a melting pot or a salad bowl. The positive attitude is that America is a melting pot in which all the people coming here from their other countries acclimate to how things are done in America. We learn to speak the same language, learn the same history, drive on the same side of the street, I would hope, and fight in wars next to each other. As such, we melt together, and when something is melted together, you cannot unmelt it. If you left a sixty-four pack of Crayola crayons in the sun in their box and they all melted under the heat, they would combine into some indescribable jumble of crayon. And once the crayons are melted together and resolidified after the sun goes away and the temperature drops, so too do Americans congeal together. If we are here long enough, we have America in us, and we cannot be put back into the country where we came from without carrying that American attitude with us.

On the other hand, there was the competing story of the salad bowl. When you make a salad, you may add various types of lettuce and greens. Then you might cut some carrots in or tomatoes. How about some croutons, olives, cottage cheese, and a salad dressing? If you are lucky, there is some shaking Jell-O that you can throw in there. Mix it all up, and what do you have? A salad. But is it really mixed up? This is not like the crayons melting together. If you had to, you could still identify each ingredient for what it is. The radicchio can be pulled out. The tomatoes can be set aside. The croutons can be scraped off, and even the dressing could be washed off the other ingredients. If you worked hard enough, you could make a pile of each original ingredient and almost have them separated. So under the salad bowl theory, we never really combine and remain separate ingredients. That is not a good thing for the strength of our nation. It is a good thing to honor your cultural and ethnic heritage and pass it on to your children. But we are in America together, whether we were born here or immigrated here. Our union is stronger if we stay together.

Chapter 3

Indirect Path to the US Army Reserve

THE MELTING POT has made a much bigger impression on me than the salad bowl. And this was underlined while serving in the 4th JAG Detachment near Fordham Road in the Bronx as a US Army reservist. I only did five and a half "good" years and another thirteen years on the Individual Ready Reserve list in St. Louis, Missouri. The IRR is there in case of a national emergency so they have more people to call. So convinced was I of the melting pot that I designed and paid for the website CheckAmerican.com back in 2010. When I thought of the name *Check American*, I thought it was such an obvious thing that I was concerned that someone else had already taken the URL for a political purpose. Not being conversant on the internet, I felt that a .com address was the strongest. There was one operation that was *CheckAmerica* for some check cashing or check printing business. But nobody had "CheckAmerican.com." This was a surprising relief. Sometime later, something like CheckAmerican.org was created. I seem to recall that it was connected with the radio talk show host Rush Limbaugh. The idea behind that site was to write "American" down on the US Census. Since Mr. Limbaugh's people had to do a search of internet web addresses, I figured that they would have preferred to use my address of CheckAmerican.com. You would have thought they would have read my short site and would have told Mr. Limbaugh of the proposed legislation on my site. I even wrote Mr. Limbaugh through his site, but I never heard back from anyone. This *Check American* idea was stronger and better than that proposed on his site, so I thought somebody would call. Nothing. Clearly, having a census form that has "American" as the first category beats having the citizen write it in for "other." But if they saw my site, it wasn't obvious to them.

In retrospect, a reason that *Check American* is powerful is that it is part and parcel of the three Ls of life, love, liberty. Love is that we are all brothers and sisters regardless of what a census taker would previously have marked down on their census form for our race, creed, color, or ethnicity. To identify as an American is to embrace people of all different skin tones and racial backgrounds. It is unity. To say that you are "American" also underscores gratitude for life for the privilege of being an American and life as we are grateful to have every day. And America and the Statue of Liberty represent liberty for millions of people around the world who do not live in America. And I certainly hope America and the Statue of Liberty represent liberty to you.

What motivated me most to conceive of *Check American* was my brief time in the US Army Reserves. I had been a conservative and proud supporter of the United States for some time since junior high school. I had heard of the disrespect meted out to US soldiers during and after the Vietnam War. I was only a kid when the Vietnam War was still going on. It ended in 1973, the year I turned thirteen. I recall news programs that would give body counts on our side and the North Vietnamese side. There were images of jungle and green uniforms and then later came the diplomacy of Henry Kissinger, also from my hometown of Furth, Bavaria, to reach the Paris Peace Accords with North Vietnam, only to have North Vietnam breach the agreement and press the war against South Vietnam in 1975, and the United States fail to reinforce the South Vietnamese, our ally. I had heard about the draft and lotteries for the draft, which had been in my distant future in 1973. I was aware that as a male, I could become subject to the draft for the Army when I would turn eighteen, but that was half a life away in time, and the conflict ended before I entered high school. By the time I got out of law school in 1985, the respect for the military had vastly improved in America.

In fact, there was a shame for the manner in which brave soldiers had been mistreated in the United States when they came back to the United States. A law client and friend of mine, Dennis Kennealy, recounted how he would take off his uniform on returning to the United States during his service in the Vietnam War, and he would hide his uniform because of taunts, such as "baby killer." The horror of the Killing Fields of Cambodia from 1975 to 1979, where over two million citizens out of about eight million were tortured, starved, and executed by the communist Khmer Rouge following the United States withdrawal from Southeast Asia, was certainly something I was aware of. Many of our young don't even know what the "Killing Fields" refers to thanks to the sanitization of our curriculum by the Academy for anything negative as relates to socialism and communism.

I had always wanted to be a lawyer since I was about fourteen. My two grandfathers had been attorneys in Germany, and I was interested in politics, and many politicians are trained attorneys. That meant after high school, I would go to college and then, if everything worked out, continue to law school after graduating from college. Things did work out, and I continued from high school, did four years of college, and then three years of law school. I received my juris doctorate from Duke University School of Law in 1985. By that time I was twenty-five. The concept of joining the army to give back to this great nation was not even on my radar screen. Usually, you might go into the service as a younger man or woman, become an enlisted soldier or do Reserve Officer Training at college, but I don't recall whether Middlebury College even supported such an endeavor, not because of politics, but there just may not have been enough interest. Besides, not that many people from Greenwich, my age, were joining the armed services. I am sure there were some from my 950 people strong senior class, but it was not an ordinary topic for conversation.

After graduating from law school in 1985, I took a four-week tour across America in my convertible, International Harvester Scout, with my good friend Andy, who had graduated from the University of Pennsylvania School of Law. We both had a one-month hiatus until the serious study for the bar exam would commence. I still maintain he could have gotten us killed in Yellowstone National Park when he belittled the potential danger from grizzly bears. I had read about it and was cognizant not to bring any food into or have any food near our tent. He mocked the threat of grizzlies even though the campground had "bear-proof" metal containers to put your food in to resist the powerful paws and jaws of the bears. He did consent to tie our food in a bundle and pulling it up into a tree to be above a potential bear's reach at night. But Andy, the Eagle Scout, Andy the Adirondack Mountain Hiker, did not put much credence in a danger from bears, so he had no problem wiping the blade of his knife on his pants during cooking over the camp stove. These were the same pants that he would bring into the tent to sleep. I was aware that if a bear were to come "into" the tent, the bear would not be knocking, and even a titanium-reinforced zipper was not going to stop a bear from coming in. And when a bear is at such close quarters, he or she is not going to distinguish between which idiot has peanut butter or other food smeared on his pants and which doesn't. The bear will go for one, the other, or both. So I slept with half an ear and half an eye open.

Now Andy had been a disappointment to his parents. He was the oldest of four boys, and like his younger siblings, he did very well in school and played on the varsity soccer team. Now on Andy's side, his father and a long line of forbearers had gone to Princeton. In fact, they had been going to Princeton before it was even founded. So obviously, he would go to Princeton. No, he would choose a different path and chose another Ivy League school, Dartmouth College in New Hampshire. Andy's decision to go to Dartmouth ruined it further for his parents because that made his next two brothers, Tom and David, go to Williams College, one of the finest small liberal arts colleges in the world, and then his youngest brother Jeff went to Dartmouth. So because of Andy, no child of his parents went to Princeton, and he topped it off by going to a top ten law school, the University of Pennsylvania. Andy and I had met in our high school Latin class, but he always did better academically. And to add insult to injury, he went out with the one girl at the high school whom I liked and idolized the most, Cece.

We started the wilderness segment of our trip to Yellowstone Park because it was the furthest East of the major National Parks. Our hiking in Yellowstone was somewhat limited because of the snowpack that was still melting off in parts of the park in May. But at Yellowstone and other parks, like Yosemite National Park in California or at the Cascades National Park in Washington State or Olympic National Park, I would keep a running dialogue going on hikes, such as "Hello, mama bear, we are just coming around the corner." I would whistle, and I even recall that we were supposed to have a bell with us to jingle. The point is not to aggravate the bear but to let the bear know that you are coming so that there are no surprises, and Mama Bear can get her cubs out of there. Well, all this noisemaking, whistling, and bells were too much for Eagle Scout Andy. He wanted the peace, quiet, and serenity of the great outdoors. He was a big hiker and was finally in the beautiful national parks of the Western United States. Why would he want some flatlander like me to ruin a beautiful hike through the woods? It would be more serene if it were quiet. So Andy, the Ivy Leaguer and top ten law school graduate, would hike some distance behind me out of ear-shot so that he would not have to listen to my constant chatter and bells and he could have the serenity of the woods. Now I grant you that perhaps he benefited from my clearing the way before us with my noisemaking, which was what the literature and rangers recommended. I am happy to say that we made it through Teton National Park, Yellowstone, North Cascades State Park, the Olympic National Park, and Yosemite in one piece.

He was an Eagle Scout, but it was clear they had not taught bear safety to Andy. By the end of our hiking, Andy had a revelation: in bear country, you should not take food with you into your tent! At least he learned it at some point and could volunteer that information to others. So even if you go to an Ivy League school, you can still learn.

On our drive back to the East Coast, we set a *Guinness Book World Record*. We put the top down on the International Harvester

Scout in Southeastern California, not far from the delicious buffets in Las Vegas, and kept the top down all the way back to Durham, North Carolina, and that included a hot spell of 106 degrees through Texas to San Antonio and Houston and the warm moist air of Mobile, Alabama, where we visited a classmate from Duke. Then after the one-month bar review class in Durham and two more weeks of bar exam studying in Connecticut, I passed the multistate bar exam and the state bar exams for New York and Connecticut. Only then could I be admitted to the bar. But before I started my job at Lunney & Crocco, a small commercial litigation firm at 640 Lexington Avenue in Manhattan, I headed off to the other side of the world to do some traveling. As my parents had said, "You don't know what it is like to live in a dictatorship unless you have lived in a dictatorship, so go visit some before they are gone."

Since I had studied three semesters of Russian as a junior and senior at Middlebury College, it was only fitting that I should try to use it in Russia, which, at the time, was run by the Communist Party and was known as the Union of Soviet Socialist Republics. And I love trains, and this was an opportunity to do the seven-day train ride from Beijing, China, all the way to Moscow. And since I never knew when I would be back on the other side of the world, I should work in some time in Communist China as well. Things were changing in China in 1985. China, after all, was home to an ancient and significant Chinese culture. It would be an interesting contrast as Deng Xiaoping had been liberalizing China, and the Chinese economy was starting to grow more rapidly and crawl out of Mao's subsistence economy. After this trip around the world, work would begin at Lunney & Crocco, so there was no room to join the armed forces for me.

Lunney & Crocco was a commercial litigation practice at Fifty-Fourth Street and Lexington Avenue in Manhattan. The principals were Robert Lunney and Charlie Crocco, both alumni from a white-shoe law firm, Shearman & Sterling. This connection helped the firm get some of its litigation work for banks and brokerage houses. That was all well and good, and after starting to work for Lunney & Crocco in the fall of 1985, I learned of the US Naval Reserve. Who knew that you could be a civilian but also a member of the military at the same time? That's pretty neat. Mr. Lunney would rush out of the office to get to his naval reserve meetings, which happened to be on Governor's Island off the southern tip of Manhattan. That was a little romantic that as naval reservists, they would take a ferry to where they would hold their drills. Sometimes there would be a formal event, and he would have his dress blues on which are quite impressive because the navy has the most elegant uniforms. Traditionally, when there were just the army and the navy, the upperclassmen would go into the navy and bring their sartorial tastes with them. Dress blue navy uniforms look quite natural in black tie settings.

I was with Lunney & Crocco from the fall of 1985 until the spring of 1988. They let me go after the Black Monday stock market crash in October 1987 but were very decent to me and let me continue working whilst I tried unsuccessfully to move from commercial litigation to general corporate. Instead of continuing my job search, I took this opportunity to head back to the Far East to travel as a backpacker in Thailand, Hong Kong, Singapore, Peninsular Malaysia and Sarawak on Borneo, Burma, Indonesia, Australia, New Zealand, and then back to China to catch the seven-day train ride from Beijing to Moscow.

During the time that I worked at Lunney & Crocco, I learned that Mr. Lunney's maritime experience had come from being in the merchant marine during the Korean War. Not insignificantly, but he also participated in the evacuation of soldiers and civilians escaping a Chinese counterattack against the United Nation forces during the Korean War, known as the Battle of the Chosin Reservoir.

What was the Korean War? It is a forgotten war in America and was the product of the Russian/Soviet imposition of a communist regime on occupied peoples. The Soviet Union had only entered the Second World War against Japan on August 8, 1945, two days after the atomic bombing at Hiroshima and six days before the surrender of the Japanese on August 14, 1945. So Russia, as is her custom, grabbed some land from Japan on Sakhalin Island north of Japan. Pursuant to the Yalta Conference with the United States and Great Britain in January 1945, the Soviet Union was to occupy North

Korea above the thirty-eighth parallel, which had been a Japanese colony since 1910. Once in North Korea, the Russians facilitated North Korea's enslavement under communism. As is the aggressive nature of communists, North Korea invaded South Korea in June 1950. Although there has been an armistice, there has never been a peace treaty to end the Korean War.

After the United Nations forces, led by the United States, pushed the North Koreans toward the Chinese border, the People's Liberation Army of Communist China counterattacked the United Nations forces on October 19, 1950. During a seventeen-day battle near the Chosin Reservoir, 30,000 United Nation forces battled approximately 120,000 Chinese troops in freezing cold weather. The United Nations forces broke out of their encirclement at the Chosin Reservoir and battled toward the port of Hangnam, North Korea, where my boss, Robert Lunney, served on a ship and was part of the "greatest evacuation movement by the sea in US military history." About 193 ships evacuated, not just the UN soldiers but also equipment and civilian refugees.[1] This is what my boss had been a part of, and he continued serving the United States in the naval reserve for decades after.

I had a great love for America, and I guess, some people might say, "Put up or shut up." And we were still locked in the Cold War with the Soviet Union in 1988. President Ronald Reagan had done much with Congress to strengthen our military after being elected president in 1980, but the Warsaw Pact was still intact and faced NATO forces in Europe in 1988. I had seen US troops in West Germany many times when I had visited over the years. I had seen the barbed wire fences, raked sand paths, and the watchtowers of the East Germans at the border with West Germany and had even been on the inside of East Berlin and had seen Soviet troops in East Germany. Based on the example set by my boss, Mr. Lunney, it would be the right thing to join the US Army Reserve. If a big conflict were to come, it would be the best way to help preserve Western democracy. So I decided to become a lawyer in the reserves as Captain Lunney

---

[1]   Wikipedia.com, *Battle of Chosin Reservoir*, accessed April 20, 2020

was a lawyer in the naval reserves. After a few phone calls, I learned that the Navy, Marines, and Air Force would only take lawyers who had had active duty experience in their branches to become lawyers in their reserve units. The Army, on the other hand, would take civilians into the US Army Reserve. It wasn't a bad trade for the Army. They received lawyers who had seven years of college and law school training without paying a cent. I would get a direct commission as a first lieutenant. So I applied and was interviewed by someone at the 4th JAG Detachment in the Bronx. A thorough physical was required as part of the application process. But before I could learn the result of my application, I left in June 1988 to travel in the Far East. Only after I came back did I learn that my application had been rejected as I had psoriasis of the skin that was on a list of disqualifying ailments. Psoriasis meant that in dry weather and under stress, cracks would develop in my fingers. So I still wanted to join. What were my options? You could appeal the denial, which I did, and they let me in.

Chapter 4

Reserve Duty Begins

WELL, I HAD to get my uniform somewhere, so I drove to Fort Devens in Massachusetts and went to a commissary to get my BDUs (battle dress uniform). That is the camouflage uniform. Then there are class A and class B uniforms for office work. Class A is more formal with a jacket and tie. The 100 percent polyester slacks and jacket are very practical. The class B uniform is the same as the class A uniform but no tie if you wear the short-sleeved shirt with a white T-shirt underneath and no jacket. I did manage to get a speeding ticket in the short distance between the entrance gate and the commissary as I exceeded the twenty-five-mile-per-hour speed limit by five miles per hour. That was my first and last speeding ticket on a military base. What better way to train military police than to enforce the driving rules on base? And this is the army—you need to follow the rules.

By the time I became a reserve officer, I had already opened my own law practice in Old Greenwich, Connecticut, in June 1989. Do you remember the advertisements that reserve duty is a part-time job, one weekend a month and two weeks in the summer? Well, at the 4th JAG, we met three Wednesdays a month and one full Saturday. Two of the Wednesday nights were in uniform, where you would get paid; and one was an administrative evening, where you would come in civilian clothes and not get paid; and then on Saturday, it would be a full day, and you would get paid. The two-week annual trainings or "AT" were done by a soldier individually or with a few members of the 4th JAG. But before all this fun, I had to do a two-week crash course in the Army at Fort Lee in Virginia. It was educational. We had to learn how to put our gas masks and chemical warfare outfits on in a specified time frame. We disassembled, cleaned, and reassembled M16 rifles. We fired the rifles on the range and zeroed our sights. We did physical training together early in the morning. We did reconnaissance through the woods with compasses and paces. We did problem-solving in small units of trying to get over a barrier with some logs and ropes. I think there were some obstacle courses to climb over. We got to fire inert, rocket-propelled grenades mounted under our M16 rifles. We got to eat meals ready-to-eat, which are also known as MREs. I liked them. They were meals in plastic pouches that could last a long time and give you a balanced meal, completed with mini Tabasco sauce bottles or candy bars. We learned the expression in the Army of "Hurry up and wait," which means you need to be at a particular place at a set time. Once you get there, things didn't necessarily begin when they were supposed to, but that was beside the point.

I was very fortunate to be a member of the 4th JAG that had produced about two generals to that point, which was pretty good for a reserve unit, but has subsequently produced many more generals. Lawyers are generally good with paper and figuring out the administrative state, which is what a big bureaucracy like the army is. The 4th JAG already had a relationship with the Staff Judge Advocate office in the US Panama Canal Zone. They later developed a relationship with the Staff Judge Advocate Office in Kaiserslautern, West Germany. This benefited officers and enlisted alike as we could take annual trainings in the US Panama Canal Zone and later West Germany. Imagine that with military orders, you didn't even need a passport to fly commercial into Panama as long as you had your orders and your military ID. The same held for traveling to Germany.

Slowly, the Army trained you to do things that were useful for soldiers. There were things called reports of survey that might bring financial responsibility for lost or damaged government property to an individual soldier. JAG officers would be involved in three different phases. There was the JAG officer that would inquire as to whether the loss or damage of government property was proximately caused by the soldier. There was the JAG officer assigned to help the soldier defend against the imposition of responsibility or at least mitigate the responsibility. And if responsibility was found, a third JAG officer would review the file for and against the soldier to see whether the requirements of a report of survey were duly satisfied all before a senior officer to the soldier imposed a financial penalty on the soldier if he or she had been found responsible.

Of great significance were drug separation boards. Doing illegal drugs is not consistent with proper military order. When I was in the service, we would have urine screening from time to time. If your urine came up positive for the metabolites of marijuana or cocaine, the army would process you for separation with less than an honorable characterization. Obviously, this can impact a soldier's job prospects in the civilian economy. As a young lieutenant, I was first assigned to assist the recorder. The recorder was the equivalent of a prosecutor. Then later as a lieutenant and captain, I was assigned to defense counsel, where we would defend the soldiers at drug separation boards. Often, a soldier who peed hot would agree to leave the reserves voluntarily, but many times, a soldier contested the results. I took it quite seriously and researched the law from Army court-martials as well as the Army regulations governing separation boards. The conduct of the boards included direct examination and cross-examination of witnesses. I prepared briefs to support motions against the government's case and their chain of custody of the urinalysis samples, amongst other issues. It was good training for our civilian legal practice.

One of my earliest assignments was to consolidate the results of a toll survey that had been completed by reserve soldiers in the 77th Army Reserve Command. The purpose had been to see whether the politicians could somehow abate the tolls the reservist paid to get over various bridges in New York City. The person who directed me was Lieutenant Colonel William Pohlmann, a very affable officer. He died in the Twin Towers terrorist attack on September 11, 2001. Our unit recognizes him as a fallen soldier of the 4th JAG Detachment.

When my father worked for a German metals company in West Germany and the United States, he had a civilian position with the North Atlantic Treaty Organization (NATO) for the procurement and acquisition of metals in wartime. That made sense since he was involved in planning and developing the mining and refining of nonferrous metals, which is basically all metals but steel. And West Germany and the United States were both in NATO together. When my father became a US citizen in 1974, he had to resign that position on behalf of West Germany. But then, the United States asked him to resume the same position but now as a citizen and representative of the United States.

Another "adventure" offered by the Army Reserves was range fire. That is where we would train on M16 rifles. Granted, there are shooting ranges where civilians can shoot rifles, or they can shoot them on their own land. And today, you have people who have paintball fights and competitions. But those are recreational. When you do range fire, you are with actual soldiers, on an actual army base, in an actual army uniform, instructed by actual army personnel on how to shoot a rifle, which is a basic skill that a soldier should have, even a lawyer. Range fire was usually a long three-day event at Fort Dix, New Jersey. We stayed in bunkhouses. The majors and above stayed in better housing. While lieutenants, captains, and enlisted soldiers would qualify on M16 rifles, the majors and above would qualify with handguns on a different range. The ranges were pretty neat because they would have pop-up targets at 50', 100', 125', and so on hidden in the woods, complete with helmets and uniforms. One evening, we even did night fire with red tracer rounds for every third bullet. Before returning to the Bronx, we had to clean our dormitory, toilets, and showers as there was no cleaning service. That was special. And it better be clean. And in the field, every rifle that was issued had to be returned, or else the whole unit would have to go looking for it. And we rode the bus together from the Bronx to Fort Dix and back. The reason I drag you through these highlights and lowlights of my time in the Army Reserves is the fact that enlisted and officers, men and women, whites and blacks, Hispanics and Asians, native born, as well as immigrants, all served together.

We all wore the army green. We all showed up together and worked together as brothers and sisters. It had been a big deal to allow blacks to fight in the Union Army during the Civil War. In fact, blacks had to continuously ask the president and Congress to allow blacks to fight and die alongside white soldiers. When referring to the 54th and 55th Massachusetts colored regiments, Frederick Douglass entreated that "the wise thing for the colored man to do was to get into the army by any door open to him, no matter how narrow…"[2] Henry Ossian Flipper was the first African American to graduate as Second Lieutenant from West Point in 1877. And it took until an executive order by President Harry Truman to integrate the US Army. But here we were, an *army of one*. (Now that too was an advertising slogan, but not in the sense that I just wrote it.)

---

[2] *Secession and War,* Autobiographies, The Library of America, New York, p. 781

Chapter 5

How the Army Leads the Nation

MY EXPERIENCE IS that the Army is now in front of our nation in terms of integration. This is what the United States should become. Two memorable Hispanic officers in the 4th JAG were Major Martir and Lieutenant Colonel Burgos. Each was sure to have a happy smile on his face whenever I saw him. Today when I go back to 4th JAG functions or the occasional change-in-command ceremony, it is impressive to see how many more Hispanic officers there are now versus twenty years ago. And being in the Army can be economic as well as patriotic. The army offers reserve officer training for officer candidates and helps with college tuition. I was impressed by what I saw and experienced. For the three Ls of life, love, liberty, this was love as we were brothers and sisters dressed in the same green. Was everything perfect? Perhaps not but certainly ahead of the nation. So when you serve with soldiers who have been born in other countries, it is a tribute to this great land that many strive to join our volunteer army. At one 4th JAG Officers event some years ago in Manhattan, I came across a captain of Korean descent. He had been born in South Korea to Korean parents. Their goal was to live in the United States. They were able to purchase or gain entry into a country like Paraguay in South America and live there for some years, and then they were somehow able to immigrate into the United States. Both of us couldn't stop saying how awesome America was and how lucky we were to be here. I had knowledge of the communists as Germany had been divided between capitalist and free West Germany and communist and repressive East Germany. He knew capitalist and free South Korea versus communist and repressive North Korea with its gulag of concentration camps for political prisoners. Immigrant countries like the United States, Canada, and Australia are incredible and are better at assimilation of immigrants than nonimmigrant countries, such as China, Russia, Japan, France, or Germany.

In considering what the Army does right and how we as a nation can emulate it, I like to think of the commencement address given by Admiral William H. McRaven, commander of US Special Operations Command in 2014. He had been a Navy SEAL for thirty-six years. On May 17, 2014, he gave the commencement address at the University of Texas, which was recounted in the *Wall Street Journal*. He shared ten points for success. The third point was most poignant for me. Over several difficult weeks of SEAL training, which includes shivering in the cold Pacific Ocean, his class had been reduced from 150 men down to 42.

> There were now six boat crews of seven men each. I was in the boat with the tall guys, but the best boat crew we had was made up of the little guys—the munchkin crew we called them. No one over about 5-foot-5. The munchkin boat crew had one American Indian, one African-American, one Polish-American, one Greek-American, one Italian-American and two tough kids from the Midwest. They out-paddled, out-ran and out-swam all the other boat crews.... Somehow these little guys, from every corner of the nation and the world, always had the last laugh—swimming faster than everyone and reaching the shore long before the rest of us. SEAL training was a great equalizer. Nothing mattered but your will to succeed. Not your color, not your ethnic back-

ground, not your education and not your social
status.

Nothing I did in the Army was particularly onerous, and it was nothing like Admiral McRaven had to endure, but I did serve with people who had served in the Vietnam War, in Afghanistan and Iraq, and other theatres. Thank heavens we have these warriors. My greatest effort, besides writing briefs to defend soldiers in drug separation boards, was trying to run the fastest during our annual physical training test at the 4th JAG and sucking wind as I raced around the track. I was the fastest for a few years until Sergeant Mele showed up. All I could do was look at his back for the first mile and then suck wind for the second mile as he finished way ahead. And yes, he was much shorter than me! *Check American* can describe everybody who wears a uniform in the United States military. My experience in the Army Reserve showed a color-blind atmosphere. A marine had defined it as green and dark green but still green. All the same color.

I don't recall exactly when I came up with *Check American*. But my experience in the US Army made clear to me how much of a color-blind society they were creating within, and the bond of soldiers as brothers and sisters is strong. Checking "American" seems logical. Once I had come up with the concept, I mailed it to my federal representatives and state representatives, but nothing would come back. I mailed it to Congressman Peter King in Long Island as he had spoken at a JAG event. Nothing came back. I would present *Check American* on the campaign trail for governor of Connecticut in 2017 and 2018. People at Republican Town Committee meetings would like the concept, but it did not animate them. It is such an obvious idea that it should have widespread appeal. On the campaign trail, I believed that everybody at a Republican Town Committee meeting would check "American" if a government form asked their race, creed, color, or ethnicity. I would say that most unaffiliated voters would check "American," and the majority of registered Democrats would also check "American" for their race, creed, color, or ethnicity. In fact, it is only a minority of Democrats that was making the Democratic Party be the party of categories and not a party of unity.

And it is that vanguard of the Democratic Party who are less likely to check "American" for their race, creed, color, or ethnicity.

You might say, "Oh wait. The Democratic Party goes out of its way to greet all different types of Americans, whites, blacks, Hispanics, Asians, Native Americans, Hawaiian Americans, etc.," but that turns out to be theory and ends up as categories and disunity in practice.

America just had a historic president, Barack Obama, Barack Hussein Obama to be exact. His mother, Ann Dunham, was from Kansas and his father, Barack Obama Sr., was from Kenya. He had a white mother and a black father, so what was he? Born in Hawaii and raised by his mother, father, and maternal grandparents in Hawaii, Indonesia, and then in Hawaii again, Barack Obama is an American, yet that category is not offered on our census form or other government forms when we are asked our race, creed, color, or ethnicity. I recall a few times when President Obama would discuss a particular issue, he might say, "A young man who looks more like me" versus saying "black" or "African American." That was a more nuanced approach. So why is President Obama forced to choose between his father or mother in marking his race or color on a census or other form or going to the end of the list to mark "other" and writing in "American?" It would seem to me altogether fitting and appropriate that the category of "American" should be the first category.

Chapter 6

2020 Census

W_{E HAD THE} decennial census in 2020. Article 1, section 2 of the United States Constitution requires the executive branch to learn how many people are in each state. That is important to determine how many representatives to the US Congress each state will send. Two senators will, of course, come from each state. Other calculations of how much money might be sent to each state for various programs are determined from census numbers. Our census now includes racial and national origin groups, and it is up to the citizen to mark his or her boxes, but it comes up short if "American" is not one of the categories. We are certainly referred to as Americans when we work, study, and travel abroad. We speak American English versus British English. We are Americans. We spell "harbor" and "labor" versus "harbour" and "labour" of the British. We live in "apartments" and not "flats." The list could go on, but the British will happily refer to us as Yanks. They don't say a "Yank who has a little Acadian out of Canada, German, Irish, Scottish, Swiss, Welsh, Kenyan, and American Indian ancestry." "Yank" covers it. Graffiti in Central America might say "Yanqui go home." "Yanqui" refers to all of us and not that a particular Yankee should stay. So if we can be recognized as Americans, Yanks, and Yankees when we are abroad, shouldn't we be able to refer to ourselves as such when we are here? When an American soldier shows up for a military or humanitarian mission abroad, he or she is still an American soldier with an

American flag patch on his or her uniform. We are not interested in that soldier's gender, color, or place of birth.

Then senator Barack Obama stated himself in *The Audacity of Hope* that "[he] reject[s] a politics that is based solely on racial identity, gender identity, sexual orientation, or victimhood generally" (p. 15). This would lead me to believe that this historic president would support *Check American.*

I have mailed the concept of *Check American,* not once but twice to Senators Richard Blumenthal and Chris Murphy, as well as to Congressmen and Congresswomen Esty, Himes, DeLauro, Courtney, and Larson, not one of whom took the time to engage the issue with me, nor have any of the other Republican politicians that I have mailed it to or shared it with. *Check American* threatens the division pushed by the identity and politically correct politicians. I have had a subscription to the *New Republic* since at least 2017. It shows up on a monthly basis, and an article in their November 2017 issue was particularly alarming. There on page 14 was an article titled "It's the Culture, Stupid: Identity politics isn't the problem for Democrats. It's the solution." Now if you are alarmed by identity politics as anathema to America, you should be concerned. Former US Ambassador Andrew Young and former US Secretary of the Treasury James A. Baker III wrote an opinion piece in August 2017, "Identity Politics Are Tearing America Apart" in the *Wall Street Journal* on August 31, 2017: "Identity politics practiced by both major political parties is eroding a core principle that Americans are, first and foremost, Americans." They closed by quoting Martin Luther King Jr., stating during his 1965 commencement address at Oberlin College, that we must "learn to live together as brothers and sisters. Or, we will perish together as fools."

The "New Republic" article, on the other hand, spoke to the long shift of working-class whites from the Democratic Party to the Republican Party, the article doubted that the Democrats could win these voters back by a bold economic agenda since the Democrats were now reliant on "a class of very wealthy donors." "[C]an Democrats win by playing on the turf of culture and identity? The short answer is yes." And I would have to say that the political dialogue has become more divisive and intolerant since that time. Who gains from division versus unity? Who gains from more categories versus fewer categories? The goal of my DACA solution proposed for illegal immigrants is greater unity and love to embrace our brother and sister illegal immigrants who can satisfy certain criteria to be allowed a legal status to stay in the United States. In exchange, "Hispanic American" and "Asian American" would disappear as minority categories as no immigrant or offspring of immigrants should ask for any special treatment for the privilege of living in this country. This is fewer categories and greater unity. Certain elements of the Democratic Party, however, have thrived on categories as the raison d'être for the party.

I say this with caution as it has been Democrats that I know personally that gave me support and guidance during my run for governor of Connecticut. Some reviewed my papers and offered helpful editing and modifications, much of which I embraced. Reverend Dr. Boise Kimber helped me during and after my campaign, which is not to diminish my most ardent supporter during and after my campaign, Austin Clark, my campaign manager. But here is the problem that I have had as a lifelong Republican: categories are very important to some Democrats. Many of these people fancy themselves friends of the poor and dispossessed. And they very well may be, but as I will delve into in later books, the War on Poverty has decimated the family in poor urban and rural communities and has made forward economic progress for the children raised in these poor communities less likely. At the same time, the default to intervention and subsidization by the state often does more harm than good. The knee-jerk reaction of some Democrats to cap or block public charter schools for high needs black, white, Hispanic, Asian and other students or prevent vouchers for private religious and non-religious schools effectively blocks school choice for the economically disadvantaged. Public charters schools, Catholic schools, and other private schools have helped many economically disadvantaged children get a decent education that they would not otherwise have received. Yet that matters not if it does not serve the interest of adult public union members versus the defenseless young. The glowing self-confidence of some of these statists can be likened to the person who buys a membership in the Sierra Club for $25 to let the world know how much he or she loves the environment. Who doesn't? The Sierra Club says it works to protect wild places and endangered species. They work to keep our air and water clean and work toward a clean energy future. They would like to curb climate change. And lastly, they now would like to pressure politicians and corporations to ensure safe and healthy environments. The latter is a little broad but laudable. And with your membership, you get a cooler tote with the name "Sierra Club" prominently emblazoned on the tote. So if you put the Sierra Club bumper sticker on your eight-cylinder Suburban, Mercedes, BMW, Audi, Range Rover, Jaguar, Porsche, Ferrari, Lincoln, or any other status car, you are letting the world know that you love the environment despite your other carbon choices. Your conscience is clear for a mere $25 donation.

Likewise, progressives claim to be caring, and many do good works in their communities. Many are allied with public unions, and together, they are able to control some "progressive" states, such as Connecticut, New York, and New Jersey. Yet they are so generous to the state and the state employees in pay and benefits that it makes life hard for the working poor due to the resultant higher cost of living. As such, the middle class and poor leave progressive states for Republican-led growth states. It can certainly be acknowledged that the forty-fifth president made some incendiary remarks about immigrants that neither Republicans, Democrats, or unaffiliated voters would support. But let's take a small issue that reflects a bigger truth. When prisoners get out of jail, it is hard to get a job. People of color are statistically more incarcerated than people not of color. Reentry into the workforce is the most important factor for a positive life. A stagnant or slow-growing economy makes reentry more difficult. High unemployment makes reentry more difficult regardless of how much the government spends on retraining programs. If the economy is weak, the demand for ex-cons will be weak. President Trump's stronger economy and the lowest unemployment rate for African Americans and Hispanics since statistics have been kept is good for both of these communities. These economic gains were set back by the Covid-19 Coronavirus pandemic that killed regardless of nationality, gender, race, creed, color, ethnicity, or party affiliation.

In June 2016, President Obama mused on exactly how did then candidate Donald Trump plan to bring back manufacturing jobs. "What magic wand do you have?" Well, President Trump cajoled American companies not to relocate their manufacturing jobs to other countries. He also encouraged foreign companies to build plants here to assure their access to the large American market. In 2018, President Trump questioned whether bailout monies paid to General Motors could be clawed back as General Motors discussed closing auto plants in the United States ("Trump Says GM should repay us taxpayers for bailout," *Reuters*, November 28, 2018). Manufacturing jobs have been a path to decent pay for a decent standard of living for decades for those without an extensive educational background. Manufacturing jobs are also something that an ex-con can do and do well. Close to five hundred thousand manufacturing jobs were added after President Trump became president but these were subsequently reduced by the Covid-19 pandemic economic contraction. And there was no magic wand. Instead, there was a questioning of what policies can help return manufacturing to the United States. If another country is cheating in its trading policies, how can that be rectified? If there is a trade deal that is disadvantageous to the United States, can we change it? While Wall Street has outsourced manufacturing jobs to Mexico and the Far East to satisfy their shareholders and their own stock options, it has started to hollow out our manufacturing base. If you look at Germany and Sweden, they have a higher percentage of manufacturing as a percent of their gross national product versus the United States, and they run pretty persistent trade surpluses. And these countries have higher costs of living than the United States. The United States runs significant trade deficits. With a focus on trying to level the playing field, President Trump was trying to open avenues of economic advancement for all Americans. To say that another approach was going to help ex-cons more than President Trump at the time was open for discussion. The point is that there should be discussion in the pursuit of truth and not a dismissal of half the union as unapproachable.

Chapter 7

Democratic Party of Categories

AT THE TIME that the Republican Party came together in the 1850s, the Democratic Party was the majority party. But the Democratic Party was also the party of categories that it is today. Then it was slave and free. In fact, the Democratic Party, as the party of slavery, poisoned not just the politics of the South then but of the entire nation, including its churches and institutions that were forced to accommodate slave and free. Frederick Douglass described the Democratic Party in a speech delivered in Elmira, New York, on August 1, 1880, as "a party which despised the negro and consigned him to perpetual slavery; a [Democratic] party which was willing to allow the American Union to be shivered into fragments, rather than that one hair of the head of slavery should be injured."[3] So with the victory of Republican Abraham Lincoln in the fall of 1860 as president with the intention to limit the spread of slavery, the Democratic Party attempted a coup d'état to take half the union out of the United States so that the white Southerner would always be free and the slave would never be free. After years of Civil War and hundreds of thousands of dead, the Confederacy was defeated. But even then, the Democrats were not satisfied. Instead, the category that was important to them was not slave and free but now black and white. The Democratic Party was the only political party in

---

[3] *Frederick Douglass Autobiographies*, pp. 930–931

American history that instituted a military wing, the Ku Klux Klan, to deny the civil rights of American citizens through mob violence and lynching. The Democrats continued their categories with Jim Crow of separate but equal. Every Jim Crow statue in our nation is to a Democrat man or woman. Today, the Democratic Party is the party of categories with the identity politics and political correctness of their progressive wing. The vanguard of the Democratic Party are the people who call themselves "anti-fascists" and wear black clothes and black helmets and shield the identity of their faces with scarves just like the cowards in the white hoods. These enforcers deny the civil rights of American citizens through their mob violence and intimidation. When Republican Senators and Congressmen presented anti-lynching and anti-mob violence legislation at the federal level after the Civil War, the Democratic Party would block the legislation to protect the tactics of the Ku Klux Klan. That history rightly revolts regular Democrats. And the violence of "anti-fascists" should alarm present-day Democrats just as we are concerned with domestic terrorists. It concerns the Democrats that I know. Categories do not help unity.

After the Civil War, Republican legislators brought anti-lynching legislation to Congress and were repeatedly defeated by Southern Democrat filibusters. According to the Tuskegee Institute statistics, approximately 4,700 Americans were lynched between 1882–1951. Of these, about two-thirds were black. Lynching was the chief tool of the Democratic Party's military wing, the Ku Klux Klan, to exercise control. One of the anti-lynching bills was introduced by Republican Congressman Leonides C. Dyer of St. Louis, Missouri, in 1918 after the lynching of a black couple. The legislation finally passed the US House in 1920 but was defeated by Southern Democrats in the Senate. The Republican Party kept anti-lynching in their party platform from then on, contrary to the Democrats who did not have an anti-lynching plank in their platform.

So here I take exception to a libel published by then Senator Obama against the Party of Lincoln in *The Audacity of Hope*. I enjoyed reading his book as it had received positive coverage before and after his election and has been instructive on how this book should be written. But in Senator Obama's discussions on the United States Constitution, he pointed correctly to how Southern Democrats had used the filibuster in the Senate to thwart civil rights legislation in the Senate and to protect the Jim Crow laws. Senator Obama intentionally glosses over that it was Democrats blocking Republican civil rights legislation. It was Republicans who passed the Thirteenth, Fourteenth, and Fifteenth Amendments to the US Constitution after the Civil War. Republicans passed the Nineteenth Amendment to give women the right to vote with thirty-six Republicans voting in the affirmative to only twenty Democrats in the affirmative. The majority of Democrats voted either "nay" at seventeen and nine Democrats abstaining. In discussing these civil rights failures, then-Senator Obama stated that senators like Senator Richard R. Russell of Georgia "used the filibuster to choke off any and every piece of civil rights legislation before the Senate, whether voting rights bills, or fair employment bills, or anti-lynching bills. With words, with rules, with procedures and precedents—with law—*Southern* senators had succeeded in perpetuating black subjugation in ways that mere violence never could" (emphasis added). Why had Senator Obama not identified Senator Russell or Southern senators as Democrats? Because it is and was an inconvenient truth.

Now they say that the victor gets to write the history. And that is the case where the victorious party gets to color and interpret a historical event more than the losing party. And this is happening in the Academy. When I refer to the Academy, I mean colleges and universities in the United States. If you want to look up US Representative Leonides Dyer, he may be referred to as a "progressive" congressman versus a Republican congressman. How long until President Abraham Lincoln is referred to as a "progressive" president as opposed to a "Republican" president? I even looked at an American history book that I had from my study of history at Middlebury College, 1979–1982, which was *American Epoch: A History of the United States Since 1900*, vol. 1, and there already is the canceling of Republican efforts in promoting civil rights and anti-lynching and masking Democrat culpability in opposition. If the left does this long enough, the history of the Republican Party will be washed away as a civil rights party interested in the advancement of Americans and unity versus the politics of categories of the Democratic Party. And the Democratic Party will continue to evade responsibility for being the party of categories.

So in discussing the filibuster and its history in the Senate, then Senator Obama described "the shameless mythologizing that allowed Southern Republicans to rise on the Senate floor and somberly intone about the impropriety of filibusters, without even a peep of acknowledgment that it was the politicians from their states—*their direct political forebears*—who had perfected the art for a malicious cause" (*The Audacity of Hope*, p. 99. [emphasis added]). This is outrageous! The Republican Party never did nor would ever abide by the slavery, Ku Klux Klan, Jim Crow laws that were the Democratic Party. To underline this point, when the Southern Democrats ruled the South, blacks left the South to pursue better opportunities in the North. This is known as the "Great Migration." The Great Migration of blacks from the South after World War I and II was to flee rule by Jim Crow Democrats. The Republicans that then-Senator Obama was referring to are of a more recent vintage and would never abide the categories enforced by the Democrat South. And who can bear witness to that? African Americans. They are now moving back to the South now that it is run by Republicans as these new migrants to the South are voting with their feet for a more pro-family, pro-business, and lower cost of living environment. They are fleeing the suffocating taxes, regulations, and high cost of living of progressive states often run by Democrats. So it is indeed libel to use sleight of hand to walk away from the legacy of the Democratic Party, the party of categories. I do not seek an apology as seems to be the fashion of the day but a retraction. I realize the stretch of this request as President Obama was the most powerful man in the world, and he is a respected and very wealthy man today. I am just a citizen. While it is the height of politics to make your party come out ahead, it is wrong to slander the Party of Abraham Lincoln with the legacy of the Democratic Party. The whole raison d'être of the Republican Party when it was formed was to limit the expansion of slavery, then to preserve the union, and then to end slavery to recognize that we are all sisters and brothers in our common humanity. As Abraham Lincoln said in his second inaugural address on the parties to the Civil War, "[O]ne of them would make war rather than let the nation survive; and the other would accept war rather than let it perish. And the war came.... Yet, if God wills that it continue, until all the wealth piled by the bondman's two hundred and fifty years of unrequited toil shall be sunk, and until every drop of blood drawn with the lash, shall be paid by another drawn with the sword, as was said three thousand years ago, so still it must be said 'the judgments of the Lord, are true and righteous altogether.'" To then try to shift the historic record of the Democratic Party for slavery, the Civil War, the defeat of Reconstruction, the Ku Klux Klan, Jim Crow's legacy of separate but equal and lynching away from the Democratic Party by a turn of phrase is disingenuous.

So the decision for the Democratic Party is whether they will support unity and *Check American* or they will continue to be the party of categories. Then senator Obama clearly stated in *The Audacity of Hope* that he sought unity. *Check American* is the epitome of unity. You and I yearn for the same unity, an America with fewer and not more categories. Any government form that asks your race, creed, color, or ethnicity must offer the unifying category of American! It is an individual's choice.

Chapter 8

The Check "American" Legislation

"AMERICAN" SHOULD BE on the 2020 census. The category of "American" will certainly alarm identity politicians and the politically correct, who trade in faction. By introducing American as an identity, it could well become the identity of the vast majority of Americans. Unity is the antidote to the poison of identity politics and political correctness. It is the answer to Marxists and socialists who thrive on division and upheaval. It is an individual's choice.

Here is the legislation that needs to be passed at the federal, state, and local levels:

> *Whereas*, there is no color for an American as we are a people whether we were born here or immigrated here;
>
> *Now, therefore*, let it be adopted that any United States / state / local government form that requests that citizens identify their race, creed, color, or ethnicity have as the first-category American to be put in an equal or more prominent position than other categories.

The passage of this legislation will be the first day of post-racial America.

Should this legislation be an amendment to the United States Constitution?

If so, why?

If not, why not?

PETER A. THALHEIM has brought his experience from sixty years of life starting as a two-year-old immigrant coming to America in 1963 to this book. He attended K-12 public school and obtained a bachelors degree in European History and later a law degree. Admitted to the bars of the states of Connecticut and New York, he practiced commercial litigation, general corporate law and residential real estate, amongst other matters. At the same time he developed his skills as a home builder and contractor by doing some of the work with his own hands and back. He has traveled around the world visiting the Soviet Union twice before it disappeared and has visited Communist China three times in addition to his backpacking through Southeast Asia. He has also spent considerable time traveling and visiting in Europe, where he has employed his average knowledge of German, basic knowledge of French and rudimentary knowledge of Russian to get about and converse. An enthusiastic American who loves the great outdoors, he has driven across the great country of the United States numerous times.

One of his proudest accomplishments was joining the United States Army Reserve as a JAG officer after starting work in New York City as a litigator. These years in the reserves shaped what would become Check "American!" More recently, Mr. Thalheim ran unsuccessfully for governor of the State of Connecticut in 2017-18 which was inspired by the positive message of "Life, Love, Liberty" of Faith Tabernacle Missionary Baptist Church, an African-American Baptist church in Stamford, Connecticut that Mr. Thalheim regularly attends. During his campaign, Mr. Thalheim was introduced to the National Association for the Advancement of Colored People, and has since been elected to the Executive Committee of the N.A.A.C.P., Stamford, Connecticut branch, in January, 2020, a non-partisan civil rights organization.